ID646097

Fire and Flame

Elizabeth Ruth Obbard ocd
Walsingham Carmel

Printed at Darlington Carmel

FIRE AND FLAME

The *Living Flame* of St John of the Cross, slightly simplified and abridged with an introduction and illustrations by Elizabeth Ruth Obbard ocd.

The Flame is the Holy Spirit.   John of the Cross

O consuming Fire, Spirit of love, descend upon me and effect in
my soul as it were an incarnation of the Word; that I may be to
him another humanity wherein he renews all his mystery.

Elizabeth of the Trinity

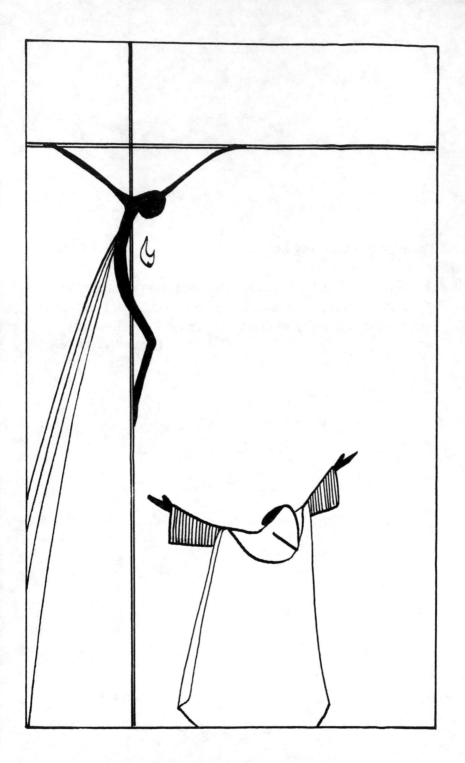

INTRODUCTION

Many people think that St John of the Cross is a writer and mystic too difficult to understand, therefore they leave him severely alone. It is true that his way of expressing himself is couched in terms not attuned to our present day conversational style, but what he has to say is perennially valid. In fact with a little effort anyone can profitably read his books and find in them a clear and unambiguous guide to the life of union with God. He is an acknowledged master of spirituality and in the *Living Flame*, short though it is, we find a complete synthesis of his teaching.

The *Living Flame* was written sometime in 1582 when John was forty years old. His trial of harsh imprisonment was behind him and he was once more restored to an honoured place in the Order. At this point he was designated to open a house of discalced nuns in Granada and after many difficulties and setbacks arrived in the city, accompanied by some of the sisters, among them Anne of Jesus with whom he had close spiritual ties, closer perhaps even than with St Teresa. The nuns went to live with a rich benefactress, Senora Ana de Penalosa, while the convent was being prepared. John expected to stay in Granada only for as long as the sisters needed him; meanwhile he took up residence in the Carmelite priory of Los Martires.

Los Martires, so called because it was situated in a former garden of conical dungeons which had been used for Christian prisoners during the Moorish occupation, was in a beautiful setting with wide views over the Andalusian countryside. In March of that year the friars of the community elected John as their superior which ensured a longer residence than he had first envisaged. The house was small and poor; John himself took on the burden of begging for alms and working as a labourer to build a necessary extension. Meanwhile he went regularly to the nuns as confessor and director.

It was at Los Martires that John completed nearly all his writings. He seemed inspired by the beautiful scenery, the peace of his surroundings, and the knowledge that he had reached the end of a difficult spiritual journey - a way of the cross which had taxed his strength, inner and outer, to the utmost. The *Living Flame* was his last work, a gift to Ana de Penalosa. He wrote it in a fortnight, fitting it in when other business was not pressing. Later he expanded and slightly amended the text, but substantially it remained the same. It is his shortest complete work and contains the fulness of his teaching and experience. In it he sketches not only the way to union with God (as in the *Ascent* and *Dark Night*) but its consummation. It is an ecstatic song of joy, the joy which follows on pain that has been endured with love.

John draws much in his commentary on the poem from the words of Scripture, revealing a special interest in the book of Esther. He draws too on the writings of St Teresa as he describes the seraph's wounding (an event immortalised in stone by Bernini). The whole work in essence can be compared to an *Exultet*, an Easter proclamation from one who has passed through death and found, not annihilation, but fulness of life. This has nothing to do with conscious feeling but with the deepest reality of the person. One has only to compare John's book with Richard Rolle's *Fire of Love* to perceive the difference. John's flame does not emit a 'felt' warmth as does Rolle's, nor is it so easily come by. The love Rolle describes is certainly fiery and passionate but it is not the result of deep purification. For example, Rolle writes:

> It is not surprising that those who have lived in God's love and are accustomed to this sweet inner burning fire are not afraid to face death but rather pass from this present life with joy. And after death they will ascend with gladness to the heavenly realms (ch. 17).

This is superficially similar to John's teaching, but there is in Rolle a facile confidence based on the *feeling* of fire and burning in the heart rather than on configuration to Christ crucified. Rolle's goal is to stir up sweetness and song within, whereas John's goal is God, attained through the dark path of the cross. Only then can one enter into the mystery of the resurrection - the consuming Flame of the Spirit who 'burns without giving pain'.

Scripturally there is a double significance in the symbol of fire. It is a revelation of the Living God and a demand for purity before him who is the all-holy One, divinely jealous for his chosen people. 'Yahweh your God is a consuming fire, a jealous God' (Deut. 4:24). Fire is an image of the intransigence of God before sin. When he comes near he must transform those whom he approaches, just as the lips of Isaiah must be cleansed with burning coals.

In Israel the sacrifice by fire, especially the holocaust where the whole of the victim was totally consumed by flames, imaged the desire for a complete self-oblation on the part of the offerer. Elijah, the prophet *par excellence*, has divine fire blaze up and accept his sacrifice upon Carmel, while he himself is as a burning torch 'taken up in the whirlwind of fire, in a chariot of fiery horses' (Sir. 48:9). The prophets are men of fire with God's word burning within them, devouring their lives in his service. Indeed, when the greatest symbols of God in the Old Testament, fire and water, are juxtaposed, it is fire, the symbol of all-consuming love, which prevails.

> Set me like a seal upon your heart,
> like a seal upon your arm.
> For love is strong as death,
> passion as relentless as Sheol.
> The flash is a flash of fire,
> a flame of Yahweh himself.
> Love no floods can quench,
> no torrents drown (Sg. 8:6, 7).

It is this strong, vital love that is the theme of the *Living Flame*, transposed into the era of Christ whose Spirit comes upon the apostles in tongues of fire. The Spirit's mission is to form the Christian into another Christ so that both share the same life-principle. The distance between God and ourselves is therefore bridged by God. Through the Spirit we share in God's own life. This is accomplished by a growing union of love. But to 'abide in love' is not natural for sinners who are self-centred. Surrender to a fiery baptism is the only way. It is this journey that John of the Cross maps out for us. If we want to give light we must endure the process of burning.

When we turn to the language John uses, we discover that it is based on metaphors we all know, or think we know well - that of human love. There is reference to gentleness, loving touch, awakening. It is the love of God the bridegroom as depicted by Hosea and Jeremiah, where Israel is the chosen wife destined to belong exclusively to Yahweh. But there is another language running parallel and equally comprehensible to us in our human condition. It is the language of devouring passion; the passion of the transcendent God who can brook no restraint. It is the language of sexual intercourse. Once passion is aroused one is swept along to self-loss in the beloved and the dissolution of ego-boundaries. Passion is a fire 'relentless as Sheol'.

Yet the *Living Flame* is tempered by gentleness. Not only is love a roaring fire, it is also glowing candles or lamps. It is the love which spends itself in silent devotion for the other even in darkness and non-feeling. It is the love of a devoted mother as well as a surrendered spouse.

The language of love is obviously that of superlatives: 'You alone are my love . . . To you I give all I have and am . . . My beloved is mine and I am his . . . I will love you forever . . . Besides you nothing else matters'. While this may sound over exclusive it is not so in reality. From a secure basis love spreads out to others; in loving the One we embrace all. This is always the fruit of choice. We may fall in love by body chemistry, we stay in love by choosing the other on a sustained basis. For the one in love with God, the fire which invades the soul warms the whole of the mystical body. As Elizabeth of the Trinity writes closer to our own times:

> In one of the psalms David sings, 'a fire shall go before him'. Is not fire love? And is it not our mission to prepare the ways of the Lord by our union with him whom the apostle calls "a consuming fire"? In contact with him our souls will become a flame of love spreading through all the members of the Body of Christ which is the Church .

While love may open the heart to the whole world, it necessarily also implies a single heart for the Beloved. Love of the One means detachment from all the rest, the closing off of other options, 'forsaking all other'. But what lover who loves with deep passion and de-

iv

votion counts the cost when placed in the scales? And was there ever a person who could love two beloveds equally? In some way there is not even a real choice, 'I can do no other'. What are wealth, possessions, esteem, honour besides love? As Paul says, 'I count everything as so much rubbish if only I can have Christ'.

Love in essence is difficult to define. We can only know its nature by considering how we express it. Of its nature love is self-diffusive; it cannot be poured into a void, there must be one who receives and reciprocates what is given. A heart to heart relationship touches us at our deepest depths. Love discovers the potential waiting to be actualised by the other who believes in us and brings to birth within us all that we can be - it is enrichment, not diminishment.

As the love of Christ was revealed above all in his death, so we must pass with him through the flame of death to resurrection and glory. In baptism we have put aside the 'old self' to be clothed in the new; thus we participate in the very life of God as Jesus promised at the Last Supper. When our baptism has been fully lived out we are in reality, not merely in symbol, united to God. Sharing one Spirit with him the soul can then give God love for love in the fullest possible way. A relationship of love can only exist where there is likeness. We have deep within us the capacity to become divine, as John of the Cross continually reiterates.

The work of the Spirit is to develop this capacity by cleansing and purifying us. This causes great pain. We have to be hollowed out for God, hand ourselves over to burning, allow him to reach into depths we cannot even guess at. Only when we are fully purified can we be transformed into another humanity 'from glory to glory'.

The *Living Flame* hymns this death and new life from the perspective of the latter. With Jesus the soul lets go of its own life, passes through a death to self and all selfish gratification, so as to receive back life in a new way, the very life of Christ. The end of the journey is not passion; that only started us on the road. The goal is reached with the gentle inbreathing of the Spirit, the kiss of love between Father and Son, in which we are called to share in deepest mystery.

In charting the path to union with God the *Living Flame* looks backwards after the goal has been reached. We will not find here a systematic exposition of the way, although John dwells on three stages of growth, all under the image of fire and flame - a stage of purification in which the soul is burned painfully so as to rid it of all impurities; a stage of transformation, when it is gradually configured to the likeness of Christ, becoming one with the divine fire; and finally the stage of union when, completely purified and transformed, the soul is united to God, sharing his life in an embrace of love.

The stage of purification must necessarily be painful, for 'as wood can never be transformed into fire if but one degree of heat necessary for that end be wanting, so the soul that has but one imperfection can never be perfectly transformed in God' as John points out in his *Ascent of Mount Carmel*. When God begins his work of love in us we will feel anguish, for we have to be detached from self and self-absorbtion. However, while love is painful before it is sweet, we must remember that it is one and the same love that manifests itself. First, it will be as a 'tough love', later, a love of gentleness. We cannot have the second if we are unwilling to undergo the first.

For John, the beginning of the spiritual journey is the generous resolve to embrace the cross. We have to really work at mortification so as to make room for God. This work, in John's terms, is the quenching of desires. It means we have to detach ourselves from running after just what *we* want rather than seeking what God wants. We blind ourselves through wanting or seeking this or that; we see events and things only as they affect us for good or ill and not as they are in themselves.

> Without mortification we shall make no progress towards perfection nor in the knowledge of God nor of ourselves . . . Neither can the darkness and ignorance of our souls be removed if the desires are not quenched . . . We are not to rely on a clear intellect or on the gifts we have received from God and then imagine that any affections and desires we may indulge will not blind us, nor cause us to fall into a worse state little by little (*Ascent*).

It takes courage to allow ourselves to die to our own way of thinking and feeling and surrender to the fire of God, letting the Spirit take over and make us other Christs, seeing, thinking and feeling as he does. Yet this does not so much need a strong will (some of us are woefully lacking in that!) but a *willingness* to yield to the demands of love. Courage is ultimately only confidence in God whose help is always present and available if we but open our hearts to receive it.

The initial push at the root of the fire of love, what enables us to take the first step, is passion. To begin to love God with passion empowers us to break away from habit and prejudice and set out on the path to holiness. We are driven towards the other by a pull stronger than our self-seeking, self-protecting natural selves. We reach out for the other, drawn irresistibly, just as the flame reaches out to draw to itself whatever is near it.

The ensuing penetration of wisdom into our souls brings light. We see more and more. We are pushed towards the fire so that love can be consummated. In the question of light John distinguishes between darkness and blindness. Blindness is culpable and proceeds from a choice of sin. We deliberately blind ourselves to areas of ourselves we do not want to see, do not want to be purified in the divine fire. Darkness, on the contrary, proceeds from ignorance. We do not even know God and the things of God and therefore do not desire them. In his own time God shows up these dark areas within us, and if we respond to the light given, we will receive further light. It is light which helps us conquer our slavery to our own desires. Desires affect our judgement and keep us in darkness; we do not see reality as it is. St Teresa in her own way says the same. If we want to do something we can find all sorts of good reasons for doing it; whereas if we do not want to do it these same reasons seem ridiculous and quite unconvincing! To admit the light into our souls is to admit reality. It is to become objective rather than subjective in our judgements, to see things from God's point of view rather than our own. Anyone who has seriously tried to do this will know it is a thoroughgoing mortification - harder than any hair shirt wearing! It is only made possible because we love another more than ourselves. It means moving *with* God rather than expending energy resisting him and trying to get our own way instead.

As we surrender, yield to the burning, we become fire, one with the fire. In this transformation the intensity of suffering is gradually overcome. A capacity for sacrifice is the proof of love, and as the desires recede so we are freed from the domination of the ego and can devote our energies to the love of God and others. For it is not that we love God and reject others. No, it is by loving them that we break the principle of seeking our own gratification. In loving others we love the God who is lover of all people.

John is truly a writer of what Bonhoeffer terms, 'costly grace'. We

THOSE WHO WOULD
GIVE LIGHT
&
MUST ENDURE
THE
BURN~
ING

cannot win God's favour, but neither does God give himself wholly to one who is ungenerous and unwilling to prove her love. This is at the root of the image of wounding which John favours. Love heals and wounds simultaneously. We can see this if we reflect on the experience of human love. It stretches us beyond the boundaries we usually place around ourselves. We find ourselves joyful at discovering that someone loves us, fearful of where it may lead. If we love another there is in some way a sense in which we are in charge; we can decide how much to give, how much to hold back. It is the wonder of discovering that we *are* loved on the other hand - we who feel so utterly worthless and unlovable - that both repels and attracts us.

> The experience of being loved and being known carries one into a new world, a world of shadows as well as of light. There is Rilke's warning: 'To be loved is to be consumed, to love is to give light with inexhaustible oil. To be loved is to pass away, to love is to endure'. [1]

In allowing ourselves to be loved by God we open ourselves to being wounded, so that he can comfort us at a level we were hardly even aware existed within us. These wounds are not necessarily spiritual in the strict sense. We are all wounded in one way or another, and through our neediness and pain we are weaned from self-sufficiency and opened to the healing power of God. This usually comes through others as we expose ourselves to them and to life, entering into the give and take of relationships. It is only if we are wounded and know ourselves to be so that we can enter into the experience of healing and redemption. As the burning and wounding reach greater depths, so we touch on the very centre of divinity within ourselves, the place where God dwells in deepest secrecy.

Only when we are perfectly purified through wounding and healing can the soul be established in grace. To love and be loved by God means facing up to demands. To return to Bonhoeffer, grace that is 'cheap' is worthless. Response to grace implies an absolute openness and obedience to all God asks. The ego has to be purged of all personal desires and 'hidden agendas'. We can certainly do part of this work, responding to the light as far as we can see, but the real work has to be done in us by God while we remain passive in his hands. John puts

[1] *The Reasons of the Heart*, John Dunne, p. 38. SCM Press 1978

it thus in the *Dark Night*.

> The soul cannot be perfectly purified . . . until God shall have led it into
> the passive purgation of the dark night . . . But it is expedient that the
> soul, so far as it can, should labour on its own part to purify and perfect
> itself, that it may merit from God to be taken under his divine care, and
> be healed of those imperfections which of itself it cannot remedy. For,
> after all the efforts of the soul, it cannot by any exertions of its own
> actively purify itself so as to be in any slight degree fit for the divine
> union of perfection in the love of God, if God himself does not take it
> in his own hands and purify it in the fire, dark to the soul.

The work of the Spirit is to reach into our depths, burn and transform
us so that we move from being children of flesh, to children of the
Spirit. He therefore makes demands on us and does not just take
possession willy-nilly.

> What the Spirit brings is . . . love, joy, peace, patience, kindness,
> goodness, truthfulness, gentleness and self-control. There can be no
> law against things like that of course. You cannot belong to Jesus Christ
> unless you crucify all self-indulgent passions and desires . . . Since the
> Spirit is our life let us be directed by the Spirit. We must stop being
> conceited, provocative and envious (Gal. 5:22-26).

For John, as for all medieval theologians, there are three areas in us
which need purification - the intellect, the memory and the will. These
are 'deep caverns' of infinite capacity which can only be filled by God.
Our task is to empty ourselves and make room for him to come in. Our
intellect, the desire to understand and grasp at God-knowledge, to
'possess' the God who cannot be comprehended, has to give way to a
vision of faith. We have to turn to the light which illumines all things
yet is not itself a graspable object of knowledge. God is too great to
be held in our tiny, cluttered minds. Clear and particular understanding must be superseded by faith, a faith held in darkness as the light
is too bright to comprehend.

Memory on its part must needs banish all daydreams, reflections,
attachments. Our memory is forever mulling over past happenings,
reflecting on what we have done or will do, wanting things and people
to be as *we* want them, avoiding them if they threaten our self-identity.
By purifying the memory, the soul is rid of useless entanglements and

preconceived opinions. Instead it is opened out to meet the future. It waits upon the future in hope and confidence, not enmeshed in any desire springing from self-love, self-aggrandisement. It waits upon the Lord in silent hope, knowing that he will make us what he wants and not necessarily what we desire. He will reveal our true being, not dependent on and held back by past experience which limits our vision.

Lastly, the will, when purified, no longer seeks dominance. It has no preference for one thing over another. It desires only to do the will of God who alone is worthy of all devotion. Selfishness in choice is thus transformed into an act of love, a giving of pleasure to the beloved Other.

This process of transformation in the 'deep caverns of sense' is long drawn out. It is like the period of espousals before a marriage is consummated. As more space is burnt out within us we become aware of untapped capacities. We feel empty and needy rather than full. We are like a girl awaiting her wedding, suddenly cognisant of a whole range of new needs and desires that will be fulfilled only when the marriage is consummated. Meanwhile she yearns for something which is not yet hers, she no longer feels complete in herself as she did when still a child. The soul likewise has to have its longings immeasurably increased so as to yearn for the fulness God wishes to give. His 'visits' to the soul, revealing as they do its inability to find fulfilment within itself, increase the longing for union with the One who alone can satisfy all desires.

In stanza three of the *Living Flame,* John makes a long digression belabouring directors who impede the soul's purification by trying to guide it according to their own ideas without being sensitive to the designs of God. There is a special need for directors to realise that in God's hollowing out of the soul's capacities there will be periods of darkness and pain. In this state the soul must be encouraged to abide peacefully in the darkness and not seek to return to sensible consolations in prayer (i.e. avoid the emptiness). It must remain in the 'dark waters' as a child carried in the womb - a metaphor used by John in the *Dark Night.*

The real nub of his advice is that we should avoid strain and effort in seeking after 'effects' at prayer; something tangible, some 'fix' or 'experience' of the God who is ultimately unknowable. This does not rule out a loving pondering on the Christ who reveals the Father to us, but it can be done in a diffuse, general way. There must be a willingness to proceed even in darkness for:

> To worship God in the light of his glory and his love is within the bounds of even a sinful man. To worship God in his impenetrable obscurity is the vocation of a saint - and we are all destined to become sanctified human beings . . . When one can worship God in the stillness of obscurity as well as in the light of his manifest presence, one has attained a level of prayer that can never cease, but proceeds from glory to glory. [1]

To contemplate is to receive, and this is impossible without silence and detachment. Detachment regarding the way of prayer is as and more important than detachment from things and people. We have to let God lead us, remaining tranquilly in a disposition that allows him to work. We should not try to bypass the desert experience of emptiness and need by filling our prayer time with useless clutter.

The main task of directors therefore is to be humble and attentive to the Lord, putting no hindrance in his way, refusing to form others according to their own pet theories. Anne of Jesus, John's disciple at Granada, when giving advice on training novices echoes his teaching by saying, 'I simply try to find out and to follow the road along which the Spirit of God is conducting a person. My own part consists merely in removing obstacles or anything which might hinder the workings of God's grace'. If we have no director or soul-friend to consult, then we ourselves can be our own worst enemy. We do not trust God to do what is best. Instead, we struggle to walk along paths we have read about or think more suitable to our temperament, rather than allowing God to carry us while we remain in his arms with perfect trust.

As our prayer progresses, as we open ourselves to the wounding and healing process on all levels, so we are drawn irresistibly to the Lord who lives in our centre. The transformed soul is like a crystal, reflecting light and indistinguishable from it. Purification brings deep peace, for the fire within burns imperceptibly like fire in the heart of the earth. It never ceases to burn, yet never consumes. This is not the peace of inertia but the peace of continual surrender. It is the end result of a long process. Paul put it this way:

[1] *The Pain that Heals.*, Martin Israel, p. 81. Mowbrays 1981

My prayer for you is that your love for each other may increase more and more and never stop improving your knowledge and deepening your perception, so that you can always recognise what is best. This will help you become pure and blameless, and prepare you for the day of Christ, when you will reach the perfect goodness which Christ Jesus produces in us for the glory and praise of God (Phil. 1:9-11).

The preparation for the day of Christ is a preparation for oneness with him, so that with and in him we may glorify the Father. John, in speaking of this oneing uses obviously sexual imagery as a way of expressing the inexpressible. Love becomes ever more insistent; nothing is allowed to stand in its way as it pursues its irresistible course. Finally, it breaks the web of bondage to all that is not God. As we are gradually divinised so we long for God more and more. We have no over-riding desire except to accomplish his will perfectly, allow him space to enter and take full possession of us. Even *now* we experience the meaning of resurrection, even here we know what eternal life is and possess it - but the price is high.

It is in the crucible of God's devouring fire that the old personality is completely remoulded so as to be divested of all its ego dominated dross. Then at last, the pearl of great price, the soul with its enshrined spark of spirit, lies revealed, and from it a new personality is born, in which the ego is a true reflection of the glory within instead of being an independent focus of domination. [1]

It is only when God has done his work that we realise we have been changed. We have become Jesus. He has 'touched' us with the purity of his wisdom which penetrates all things. The silent, attentive soul is able to discern him, rest under his 'tender hand' and 'gentle touch' if it rests in purity (i.e. without desires). 'Blessed are the pure in heart, they shall see God'.

Another image used in the *Living Flame* is that of awakening. It is related to receiving the light but refers more directly to the actuating of our potential to see. As we are purified so we perceive more about God and about ourselves. He 'awakens' us to all he is, all we are, as a man awakens a woman both to his own love, his own being, and her capacity to respond. In this we cannot awaken ourselves. The ardour,

[1] Martin Israel. op. cit. p. 129

xiii

tenderness, surrender of a woman's love (and in mystical literature the soul is always feminine to God) are discovered in response to the Other in whom are united power and love, force and tenderness, and who draws us into a union beyond anything we could imagine or initiate.

When purification is complete, when the soul is all fire, it lives and burns as one with the Holy Spirit, the Flame. Pulled by passionate love, purged by devoted love, there is now a true union of wills with God. All the soul does is under his influence. It clings to his words and works, becomes ever more like him. However, only in heaven does love alone remain. No matter how closely united we are to the Lord on earth, even in the spiritual marriage, there is always more to hope for, always further to go. There is within the soul a tender voice calling incessantly to the union which can be perfected only in death. This is not a conscious 'death wish', such a thing would not be a sign of holiness; it is rather a drawing towards God beneath the level of consciousness. A modern author writes of this as follows.

> My God is the God revealed in Jesus. It is impossible to think of him condemning me, not because I am good but because he is good and I have cast myself upon the bosom of his goodness and consented to remain always weak and poor so as to receive his love more freely. I have longed for death as the only way out, merely as an end to darkness, suffering, untold mystery. And yet deep down I have known that for me, death would mean revelation, death would mean love. Oh, so hidden away were these convictions that they afforded me no consolation on the conscious level. [1]

Union with God in the spiritual marriage is for fruitfulness. This is the significance of the Seraph's wound, the penetration of the soul which makes us burn with inner fire. It is a gift given for others. It is secret like the name on the white stone, as all love is secret and sacred between the two who share it. In fact, to try and describe what is essentially indescribable makes it sound trivial. Pierced to our depths, emptied of self, the whole world enters in to fill the vacant space. The saints are the most full themselves because emptied of self, the most compassionate of mortals because they have passed through the fire of pain and know suffering from the inside.

[1] *Before the Living God*, Ruth Burrows, p. 113. Sheed & Ward 1975

Those who are one with Jesus live outside the self and in God. Wholly burnt up in the flame of Christ, they keep a perpetual feast, secure in love and joy. They live in the world of the risen Jesus. Even if pain and suffering are present their nature is changed. Joy is present always, despite outward appearances. 'I say to the Lord you are my God, my happiness lies in you alone' (Ps. 14:1, Grail version).

Union with Christ means that in some way the soul is able to give God to God, can share in all his attributes, merge with the fire and burn with many lamps. She reflects in herself the very glory and splendour of God, for 'this is the unfathomable nature of love, that it desires equality with the beloved, not in jest merely but in earnest and truth' (Kierkegaard).

Thus the soul enters into a true matrimonial pact because she shares the same nature with the Spouse. She can love him selflessly for himself rather than for his gifts. She can thank him in an excelling manner because she has received so much so freely.

The climax for John comes in the symbol of the kiss - God's inbreathing, the mark and seal of deep marital love, the sharing of the one Spirit. For this we were made: 'Come, receive the kingdom prepared for you from the foundation of the world'.

* * * * *

But let John of the Cross speak for himself. In the following rendering of the *Living Flame* I have simplified some of the language and slightly shortened the text, but in substance it is all John's. His are the words of one who truly walked the mystical way and knew both the pain and the joy of God's purifying fire until he became one with the Flame, as he so desired.

The Living Flame of Love

The Living Flame of Love

INTRODUCTION

It is with some trepidation that I enter upon an explanation of the four
stanzas which are the subject of this treatise. This is because they
relate to matters so interior and spiritual as to baffle the powers of
language.
But now that our Lord seems to have opened the way of knowledge
and given me some spiritual fervour
I have resolved to speak.
Relying on holy Scripture
I want to share what I have learned.
Though I have to warn you that all I can say
falls far short of that which passes
in the intimate communion of the soul with God.

There is nothing strange in the fact
that God gives such great favours to people he is pleased to comfort;
for if we consider attentively
it is God himself,
a God of infinite love and goodness,
who bestows them.
For the Lord himself said
that the Father, the Son and the Holy Spirit
would come to those that love him
and abide within them (cf. Jn. 14:23)
And this is accomplished in the way I intend to describe
in the following stanzas.

When a log of wood is set on fire
and when it is transformed into fire and united with it,
the longer it burns and the hotter the fire,
the more it glows until sparks and flames are emitted from it.
So too the soul,
when transformed and glowing interiorly with the fire of love,
is not only united to the divine fire
but becomes a living flame itself
and is conscious of being such.

The soul in these verses speaks of this transformation
as it burns with the sweetness of love
and ponders over all that has been wrought within it.

O Living Flame of Love
That so tenderly wounds
My soul in its deepest core!
As you are no longer painful
Perfect your work in me if you so will,
Break the web of this sweet encounter.

O sweet burn!
O delicious wound!
O tender hand! O gentle touch!
Savouring of everlasting life
And paying the whole debt,
In destroying death you have changed it into life.

O lamps of fire,
In whose splendours
The deep caverns of sense,
Usually dim and dark,
now with unwonted brightness
Give light and heat together to the Beloved.

How gently and how lovingly
You lie awake in my heart,
Where you dwell secretly and alone;
And in your sweet breathing
Full of grace and glory
How tenderly you fill me with love.

O Living Flame of Love
That so tenderly wounds
My soul in its deepest core!
As you are no longer painful
Perfect your work in me if you so will,
Break the web of this sweet encounter.

The Spouse of Christ
feeling herself all on fire in the divine union,
feeling also that 'rivers of living water' are flowing from her
as our Lord promised to faithful souls, (cf. Jn. 7:38)
imagines that, as she is so profoundly possessed by him,
so richly adorned with gifts and graces,
only a slender veil separates her from eternal joy.
Seeing too the sweet flame of love burning within her,
she addresses herself to this Flame, the Holy Spirit,
and prays him to destroy her mortal life
and bestow upon her perfect glory.

O Living Flame of Love

O is an exclamation of strong desire and earnest supplication,
while the Flame of Love is the Spirit of the Bridegroom,
the Holy Spirit.
The soul is conscious of the Spirit's presence within it
as a consuming fire which transforms it in love.
It is as a burning fire sending out a flame
which bathes the soul in glory
and recreates it with the refreshment of everlasting life.

The Holy Spirit kindles the transformed soul,
setting it on fire
and making it one with the flame
through a union of wills - the soul's and God's.

Thus the soul's acts of love are most precious
because they are all under the influence of God
and lift the soul heavenwards.

'As your word unfolds it gives light', (Ps. 119:130)
and 'Does not my word burn like fire?' (Jer. 23:29)
We learn from the Lord himself
that his words are 'spirit and life', (Jn. 6:64)
and souls full of love feel their power and efficacy,
whereas impure souls find them insipid.

Thus when the Lord announced the doctrine of the Eucharist,
a doctrine full of sweetness and love,
'many of his disciples left him'. (Jn. 6:7)
Yet not all souls made this response;
St Peter loved the words of Christ for he replied,
'Lord, who shall we go to? You have the words of eternal life. (Jn.
6:69)
The woman of Samaria forgot the water and left her waterpots
because of the sweetness of the words of the Lord. (cf. Jn. 4:28)

Now, when the soul has drawn so near to God
as to be transformed in the Flame of Love which is the Spirit,
it has a foretaste of everlasting life.
The flame is said to be living
because it causes the soul to live spiritually in God
and be conscious of that life within it;
as it is written,
'My heart and my flesh sing for joy to the living God'. (Ps. 84:2)

That so tenderly wounds

That is, you touch me tenderly in your love,
softening and melting as the bride says in the Canticle,
'My soul melted when he spoke'. (Sg. 5:6)
This is the gift of God's words heard in the soul.

But how can God wound the soul
when it seems there is nothing left to wound,

6

all having been consumed in the fire of love?

Fire is never idle
but is always flashing first in one direction and then another.
So love, whose function is to wound,
darts forth as a living flame, wounding with love and joy,
as Christ said himself,
'I was delighting him day by day,
ever at play in his presence,
at play every day in the world,
delighting to be with the children of men'. (Prov. 8:30, 31)

This wounding is therefore the playing of divine wisdom
touching the soul continually and never idle.
And these flashings of fire wound the soul
in its deepest core.

My soul in its deepest core.

The inmost centre of a person is inaccessible
to the world, the flesh and the devil.
There dwells the Holy Spirit
who inflames and directs the soul
without any interference from the outward senses.

The centre of the soul is God.
When the soul has reached him
it will have attained to its ultimate and deepest core.
This will be when the soul shall love God,
understand and enjoy him with all its strength.
When, however, the soul is not in its deepest centre
but can move still further inwards,
it is necessary to keep advancing.

Love unites the soul with God.
The greater the love
the deeper does it enter into God
and the more it is centred on him.

There are many mansions in the Father's house. (Jn. 14:2)
Thus, even one degree of love
places us in a state of abiding grace
and therefore in God.
With two degrees of love we move closer,
with three degrees closer still, and so forth.
But if the soul has attained the highest degree of love
it will be wounded in its inmost depth
and be both transformed and enlightened.

In this state the soul can be compared to a crystal,
lucid and radiant.
The greater the light thrown on it
the more luminous it becomes
until it seems like the light and is indistinguishable from it.

The living flame in the depths of the soul
is as a 'furnace in Jerusalem'. (Is. 31:5)
Jerusalem means 'vision of peace'
and the soul in the burning furnace
is more peaceful, tender and glorious
in its union with God
the more the flame transcends the fire of ordinary love.

The divine Wisdom here absorbs the purified soul,
for 'Wisdom reaches everywhere by reason of her purity' (Wis. 7:24)
and the flame is so sweet that the soul says,
'As you are no longer painful'.

As you are no longer painful

Before the soul entered the state of union
the flame was neither peaceful nor sweet.
For its work was to purify the soul,
destroying and consuming its imperfections and evil habits.
This is the work of the Holy Spirit
who then disposes the soul for divine union
and transformation in God by love.

8

For the flame which unites itself to the soul
in the glory of love
is the very same which before enveloped and purified it;
likewise, the fire which ultimately penetrates
the substance of the fuel
is the same which in the beginning
darted its flames around it,
depriving it of its coldness and preparing it
for being transformed into fire itself.

Lord, in the joy of union with you
the Flame is no longer a cause of grief and affliction.
Rather, it is glory, delight and freedom.
I can apply to myself the words of the Canticle,
'Who is this coming up from the desert, flowing with delights
and leaning upon her Beloved?' (Sg. 8:5)
scattering love on all sides.

Perfect your work if you so will

That is - perfect the spiritual marriage in the beatific vision.
The more the soul is resigned
the more it is transformed,
knowing and seeking nothing for itself
because of its perfect love.
Yet it still lives in hope
and hope implies want.
For however intimate the soul's union with God,
here below it can never be fully satisfied.

Even so, the soul's desire is so at one with God
that it only wills whatever he wills;
yet it would seem to itself to love but little at this stage
if it did not long for the perfect consummation of love.

It is as if the Holy Spirit invites the soul:
'Come then my love,
my lovely one come.

For see, winter is past,
the rains are over and gone.
The flowers appear on earth.
The season of glad songs has come,
the cooing of the turtledove is heard
in our land.

The fig tree is forming its first figs
and the blossoming vines give out their fragrance.
Come then my love
 my lovely one, come.
My dove, hiding in the clefts of the rock,
in the coverts of the cliff,
show me your face,
let me hear your voice;
for your voice is sweet
and your face is beautiful'. (Sg. 2:10-14)

All this the soul hears spoken within it
by the Holy Spirit
in this sweet and tender flame.
And therefore it replies, 'Perfect your work if you so will'.
This is merely the two petitions our Lord commands us to make,
'Your kingdom come, your will be done'.
That is: give me your kingdom according to your will.
And so the soul continues,
'Break the web of this sweet encounter'.

Break the web of this sweet encounter.

It is an easy thing to draw near to God
when hindrances are set aside
and the webs that divide us from him are broken.
There are three webs to be broken
before we have perfect fruition of God.
The temporal web of created things,
the natural web of merely natural inclinations and actions,
and the sensitive web - the union of soul and body.

'For we know that when the tent we live in on earth
is folded up,
there is a house built by God for us,
an everlasting home not made by human hands
in the heavens'. (2 Cor. 5:1)

The first and second web must necessarily have been broken
before we reach the fruition of God.
This was done when we denied ourselves
in worldly things,
renounced our merely natural desires and affections,
and when all we did became gradually divinised.
This was accomplished by painful burning.

Now the sensitive web alone remains to be broken
and the flame assails it
with sweetness and delight.
Thus the death of such souls is sweet
for they die of the sweet violence of love,
even as a swan sings more beautifully as death approaches.
For the soul now longs 'to be dissolved and to be with Christ'.

This life is called a web
because of the connection between spirit and flesh
which separate the soul from God.
Also, as a web allows the light to shine through it,
so the divinity shines through the soul
when it has been refined in the fire.
Thus the soul comes to see things as God sees them,
to whom 'a thousand years are a single day,
a yesterday now over, an hour of the night' (Ps. 90:4)
and before whom 'all the nations are as nothing'. (Is. 40:17)
In the same way
all things appear to the soul as nothing, even itself;
God alone is all.

Why does the soul pray for the breaking of the web
rather than for its cutting or removal?

12

Because it is more natural that a thing
should be broken in an encounter
than that it should be cut or taken away.
Love is familiar with force and impetuous contacts
and breaking is quicker than waiting for natural termination.
Hence in the matter of life
the soul knows that God wishes to call some to himself
before the normal time
because love has perfected them early,
so they are admitted to see God face to face.
'He has sought to please God, so God has loved him;
as he was living among sinners he was taken up.
He has been carried off so that evil may not warp his understanding
or treachery seduce his soul . . .
Coming to perfection in so short a while,
he achieved long life;
his soul being pleasing to the Lord
he has taken him quickly from the wickedness around him'. (Wis.
4:10-14)
In encountering God
the soul is indeed assailed and penetrated
by the fire of the Holy Spirit
who deifies and perfects it.

O fire of the Holy Spirit,
penetrating so tenderly and profoundly
the substance of my soul,
I pray for the breaking of this life's web,
that I may be enabled to love you hereafter
with the fulness and abundance my soul desires,
loving without end and for evermore.

II

O sweet burn!
O delicious wound!
O tender hand! O gentle touch!
Savouring of everlasting life
and paying the whole debt.
In destroying death you have changed it into life.

We learn here that the three persons of the Trinity,
Father, Son and Holy Spirit
accomplish the work of union.
The 'hand', the 'touch' and the 'burn'
are in substance one and the same,
yet the effects are peculiar to each.
The 'burn' is the Holy Spirit,
the 'hand' is the Father,
and the 'touch' is the Son.
Here the soul magnifies Father, Son and Holy Spirit,
extolling those three gifts and graces,
which they perfect within it;
for they have changed death into life,
transforming it into themselves.

The first of these gifts is the delicious wound
which is attributed to the Holy Spirit.
For this reason the soul calls him the 'burn'.
The second is the 'taste of everlasting life'
which is attributed to the Son,
thus he is designated as the 'gentle touch'.
The third is that 'gift'
which is the perfect recompense of the soul;
this is attributed to the Father
who is therefore called the 'tender hand'.
Though these three persons of the Trinity
are referred to severally

14

because of the manner in which they work,
the soul is addressing itself to but one Essence, saying
'you have changed it into life'.
For the three divine Persons work together
and the whole is attributed to each and all.

O *sweet burn!*

Moses said, 'Yahweh your God is a consuming fire', (Deut. 4:24)
that is, a fire of love.
As his power is infinite he consumes infinitely,
burning with great vehemence
and transforming all he touches into himself.
But he burns all
acccording to the measure of their preparation,
some more, some less;
and also according to his good pleasure
as and when and how he wills.

The fire of love is infinite,
so when God touches the soul
the burning heat within it becomes so extreme
as to surpass in intensity all the fires of this world.
Hence it is a 'burn' more intense and concentrated
than that of other fires.
When the divine fire shall have transformed the soul into itself
the soul feels not only the burn
but also wholly burnt up in the vehemence of the fire.

O how wonderful the fire of God!
Though it is strong enough to burn up whole worlds
more easily than an ordinary fire destroys a single straw,
yet it consumes not the spirit wherein it burns;
but rather, in proportion to its strength and heat,
delights and deifies it,
burning sweetly within
according to the strength which God has given.

16

Thus on the day of Pentecost
the fire descended with great vehemence on the apostles
who, according to St Gregory, burned sweetly interiorly.
The Church also says of that event,
'The divine fire came down, not consuming but enlightening'.
For as the object of the Spirit's coming
is to elevate the soul,
the burning of the fire does not distress but cheers it,
does not weary but delights it,
rendering it glorious and rich.
Thus the fire is said to be sweet.

So the blessed soul,
which by God's mercy has been burned,
knows all things, tastes all things.
'Success attends all he does'. (Ps. 1:3)
Against it nothing shall prevail, nothing defile.
To such a soul the apostle referred when he said,
'A spiritual person is able to judge the value of everything
and his own value is not to be judged by others'. (1 Cor. 2:15)
For 'the Spirit reaches the depths of everything,
even the depths of God', (1 Cor. 2:10)
because it belongs to love to search into all the beloved has.

O great glory of souls
who are worthy of this supreme Fire!
It has infinite power to consume and annihilate you,
but it consumes you not
and makes you infinitely perfect in glory!
Do not wonder that God should elevate some souls
to such a height,
for he alone is wonderful in all his works.
As this burn is so sweet, how happy that soul must be
who has been touched by this fire!
It cannot explain all its joy, though anxious to do so.
So it rests satisfied with words of endearment and esteem, saying
'O delicious wound'.

O delicious wound, which he who causes relieves and heals
even while he inflicts it.
It bears some resemblance to the sterilising use of fire
which, when applied to a wound,
renders the wound a wound of fire
until all extraneous matter has been destroyed.
The healing which love brings is to wound again
what was wounded before,
until the soul melts away in the fire of love.
So when the soul shall become one great wound of love
it will then be transformed in love.
Paradoxically, the most wounded soul is the most healthy,
and whoever is all wound is all health.

Even if the soul has become one wound, and consequently sound,
the divine burning does not cease but continues to burn.
Its work, though, is also to soothe the healed wound
and thus the soul cries out, 'O delicious wound',
the more delicious the more penetrating it is.

The Holy Spirit himself inflicts the wound
that he might soothe it.
Thus he inflicts a great wound in order to comfort abundantly.

O blessed wound inflicted by him who cannot but heal it!
O happy and most blessed wound!
You are inflicted only for the soul's joy and comfort.
Great is the wound because of the greatness of its Inflictor.
Great is the delight of it, for love's fire is infinite!
O delicious wound;
the more delicious the more it penetrates the soul's substance,
burning all it can burn,
that it may supply all the delights it can give.

This burning and this wound, in my opinion,
are the highest condition attainable in this life.

There are many other forms of burning
but they neither reach so far nor are similar to this;
for this is the touch of the Divinity
without form or figure.

But the soul is burned in another and most excellent manner
when it is on fire with love,
(though not in the same degree as formerly mentioned).
Here it will feel as if struck by a Seraph with burning brand
who penetrates it as fire and flame on glowing coals,
cauterising it all at once.
In the very act of cauterisation
the flame rushes forth and surges vehemently,
as fire and flame revive and ascend
when burning fuel is disturbed.

In this state the soul feels that the wound is perfect,
for it feels the depths of its spirit transpierced
with a delight more exquisite than words can express.
The soul feels, as it were, a minute grain of mustard seed
pungent and burning in its inmost heart - the spot of the wound,
and from there it diffuses itself
through all the spiritual veins of the soul.
It feels its love growing, strengthening and reviving itself
to such a degree that it seems to the soul
that it is as seas of fire overflowing with love.

The feeling of the soul at this time can only be described
by saying that it now understands
why the kingdom of heaven is compared to a mustard seed,
which by reason of its inherent natural heat
 grows into a lofty tree. (cf. Matt. 13:31, 32)

The soul beholds itself now as an immense sea of fire.
Few souls, however, attain to this state,
but some have done so,
especially those whose spirit and power
is to be transmitted to their spiritual children.

They are a kind of 'first fruits',
since God bestows on a Founder such gifts and graces
as are commensurate with the importance of the Order.

To return to the work of the Seraph - which is to wound.
Maybe the inner wound will be manifested exteriorly
as with St Francis;
for when the Seraph wounded his soul with love
the effects became outwardly visible in the stigmata,
for God confers no favours on the body
which he does not confer chiefly and primarily on the soul.
In that case, the greater the joy and violence of the love
which caused the interior wound,
the greater will be the pain of the visible wound;
and as the former grows so does the latter.
This is because such souls delight in the strong Spirit of God
who, however, causes pain in weak and corruptible flesh.
Thus it is a marvellous thing
to feel both pain and sweetness together.

O infinite greatness in all things!
You, Lord, cause sweetness in the midst of bitterness,
pleasure in the midst of pain.
O delicious wound!
The greater the delight the deeper the wound.
But when the wound is in the soul alone,
and not communicated to the body,
it is the more intense and keen.
For the flesh checks the spirit and restrains its course,
'for a perishable body presses down the soul,
and this tent of clay weighs down the teeming mind'. (Wis. 9:15)

Whoever, therefore, trusts too much to bodily senses
will never become a very spiritual person.
I say this for the sake of those
who think they can attain to the heights of the spirit
by the mere energy and action of the senses.
Yet we cannot become truly spiritual at all

unless the bodily senses be restrained.
It is quite different when things happen the other way around
and the spirit flows into the senses;
for there may be great spirituality in this
as in the case of St Paul,
whose deep identification with Christ's sufferings
overflowed in his body and who said,
'The marks on my body are those of Jesus'. (Gal. 6:17)

O tender hand, O gentle touch.

O hand as generous as you are powerful and rich,
O gentle hand laid so gently upon me!
And yet, if you were to press at all the whole world would perish;
for at the very sight of you the earth trembles,
the nations melt,
and the mountains are crushed to pieces.

O gentle hand, hard and heavy when you touched Job
but to me loving, gentle and gracious!
You are as sweet and gentle to me
as you were hard and rough to him;
the tenderness with which you touch me
surpasses the severity with which you touched Job.
You kill and give life - no one can escape your hand.

But, O divine life,
you never kill except to vivify,
you never wound except to heal.
O divine hand - you have wounded only to heal me.
You have slain in me that which made me dead
and have made me live instead the very life of God.
This you have wrought in the liberality of your grace,
through your touch - that touch
which is the 'brightness of your glory,
the perfect copy of your nature', (Heb. 1:3)
your only begotten Son, in whom, being Wisdom itself,
you 'reach from one end of the earth to the other
ordering all things for good'.

22

O gentle touch - O Word, the Son of God,
who, because of the pureness of your nature
can penetrate the very substance of my soul,
touching it gently, absorbing it wholly.
O touch of the Word,
so gentle, so wonderfully gentle to me;
and yet you were 'overthrowing the mountains
and breaking the rocks in pieces' at Horeb.
But then you announced your presence to the prophet
by the sound of a gentle breeze. (cf. 1 Kgs. 19:12, 13)
O gentle air, how is it you touch me so gently
when you are terrible and strong?
O blessed soul, most blessed,
which you, O strong and terrible Lord
touch with such gentleness.
Proclaim it to the world, O my soul.
But no - proclaim it not,
for the world knows not the 'gentle breeze',
neither will it listen to it
for it cannot understand matters so deep.

O my God and my life,
they shall know and behold you who,
making themselves strangers on earth, purify themselves,
for purity corresponds with purity.
The more gently you touch the more you are hidden
in the purified souls of those who have made themselves strangers,
hidden on earth from the face of creatures,
and whom you 'shelter inside your tent
far from the war of tongues'. (Ps. 31:20)
O again and again, gentle touch,
which removes the soul from all other things
and makes it entirely your own;
you leave behind impressions so pure
that the touch of everything else seems vile and worthless.
You are subtle and diffused, spreading and filling the soul.
And now, because you have touched it, the vessel of my soul
is pure and clean and able to receive you.

O gentle touch!
as there is nothing material in you
so the more profoundly you touch me,
changing what is human in me into what is Divine;
since you touch me with your very self,
free from all that can affect the senses.
Finally, then, O gentle touch,
O most gentle;
you touch me with your simple and pure essence
which, being infinite, is infinitely gentle.
For this reason it is a touch so subtle, loving,
surpassing and delicious.

Savouring of everlasting life

What the soul tastes now in the touch of God
is in some way a foretaste of everlasting life.
It is not incredible that this should be so
when we believe that the touch is such
that the substance of God touches the substance of the soul.

Many saints have experienced it in this life
and the sweetness occasioned baffles all description.
Neither can I speak of it
lest people suppose it is nothing beyond what my words imply.
Indeed there are no words to describe the deep things
God brings to pass in perfect souls.
Let the one who has been favoured with them
judge them, feel and enjoy them by himself,
and be silent about them.
For the soul sees that they are in some measure
like the white counter of which it is written,
'To those who prove victorious I will give . . . a white stone,
a stone with a new name written on it,
known only to the one who receives it'. (Rev. 2:17)

Though as yet the fruition of God's touch is not yet perfect
it may truly be said to be 'savouring of everlasting life',

for the soul tastes in a marvellous manner, and by participation,
of all the things of God -
fortitude, wisdom, love, beauty, grace and goodness
all being communicated to it.

And as the soul tastes of such great good
some of the Spirit's unction overflows occasionally in the body
as it is written, 'All my bones shall exclaim,
"Yahweh, who can compare with you?" ' (Ps. 35:10)

And paying the whole debt

What debt then does the soul refer to
as being paid or satisfied? It is this.
Those souls who attain to the high state of spiritual betrothal
have generally passed through many tribulations and trials
because, 'We all have to experience many hardships
before we enter the kingdom of God'. (Acts 14:22)
And these tribulations are now passed.

What they have to suffer
who are to attain to union with God
are divers afflictions and temptations of sense,
trials, tribulation, temptations, darkness and distress of mind,
so that both flesh and spirit may be purified together
(as I have described in my treatise of *The Ascent* and *Dark Night*).
The reason for this
is that the joy and knowledge of God
cannot be established in the soul
if the spirit and flesh are not perfectly purified and refined.

And as trials and penances purify and refine the senses,
as tribulations, temptations and darkness
refine and prepare the spirit,
so those who wish to be transformed in God
must undergo sufferings;
just as those in purgatory attain to the Beatific Vision,
suffering more or less intensely,

for longer or shorter periods,
according to the degree of union to which God intends to raise them
and according to their need of purification.

It is by trials to which God subjects the spirit and the flesh
that the soul acquires virtues and fortitude and perfection.
These are bitter experiences, for the apostle says,
'My power is at its best in weakness'. (2 Cor. 12:9)
For virtue is made perfect in weakness
and refined in the context of the passions.
Iron can only be fashioned to the artist's pattern
through the use of fire and hammer,
and during the process its previous condition is injured.
This is the way of God's teaching, as the prophet says,
'He has sent fire from on high
down into my bones'. (Lam. 1:13)
He speaks of the hammer too where he says,
'You have disciplined me and I accepted discipline;' (Jer. 31:18)
so too the Wise Man says,
'What does he know who has not been tried?' (Eccl. 34:11)

People ask why so few ever attain to this state.
The reason is, that in this marvellous work
which God himself begins, so many are weak,
shrinking from trouble, unwilling to endure discomfort,
unwilling to labour with constant patience.
Hence God, not seeing them diligent in cultivating the graces
he gave when he began to try them,
proceeds no further with their purification,
for it required greater courage and resolution than they possessed.
We are therefore to count it a great favour
when the Lord sends us exterior and interior trials,
remembering that they are few in number
who deserve to be made perfect through suffering.

Those souls who do attain to this high estate
obtain all their desires.
They were as Modecai weeping in the streets of Susa

26

because his life was threatened,
clothed with sackcloth and refusing the garments sent by Esther,
unrewarded for his faithful service in defending the king's honour.
Yet he found that his trials and service
were rewarded in one day.
Like him, the faithful soul
is not only admitted within the palace
and stands before the king clothed in royal robes,
but also wears a diadem and carries a sceptre,
and sits on the royal throne with the king's signet ring on its finger,
symbols of its power in the kingdom of its Spouse.

Even so, the soul's enemies which sought its life are dead,
while it now lives in God.
'In destroying death you have changed it into life'.

In destroying death you have changed it into life.

There are two kinds of life:
one beatific, consisting in the vision of God.
This must be preceded by bodily death, as it is written,
'For we know that when the tent we live in on earth is folded up,
there is a house built by God for us,
an everlasting home not made with human hands, in the heavens'.

(2 Cor. 5:1)

The other life is the perfect spiritual life,
consisting in the possession of God in a union of love.
We attain to this by mortifying our evil habits and desires.
Until we do this, perfect union with God is unattainable,
'For if you obey your unspiritual selves
you are doomed to die;
but if by the Spirit you put an end
to the misdeeds of the body
you will live'. (Rom. 8:13)

By 'death' here is meant putting an end to 'the old man',
to employing our faculties in useless desires

28

and wasting ourselves on created things.
Rather, 'You must put aside your former self . . .
Your mind must be renewed by a spiritual revolution
so that you can put on the new self
that has been created in God's way,
in the goodness and holiness of truth'. (Eph. 4:22, 24)
In this new life of perfect union with God
all the acts and affections of the soul,
which in themselves are as it were imperfect, become divine.
For our actions show who we are,
and if we live and act with the mind of God, in union with him,
we do indeed live with his very life.
Death has been changed into life.

The intellect is now illumined by God,
the will loves deeply, loving with divine love
and moved by the Holy Spirit,
the memory keeps in mind 'the eternal years'.
The desires which previously longed for created food
now taste and relish what is divine.
Finally, all the motions and acts of the soul
which proceed from its natural and imperfect life,
are changed, through union with God, into divine acts.
For the soul is now the true child of God,
and is moved by the Spirit of God, as it is written,
'Everyone moved by the Spirit is a son of God'. (Rom. 8:14)
The soul is obviously not God
but by its union with him really participates in his life.

The soul can therefore say with St Paul,
'I live now not with my own life
but with the life of Christ who lives in me'. (Gal. 2:20)
What in the soul was dead and cold is fully vivified
by contact with the life of God.
Thus are fulfilled the words of Scripture,
'Death is swallowed up in victory', (1 Cor. 15:54)
and, 'O death, I will be your death'. (Hos. 13:14)

The soul is now able to be led into the chamber of the King
where it rejoices in the Beloved
whose 'love is more delightful than wine';
while it says, 'I am black but lovely, daughters of Jerusalem', (Sg.1:2,5)
for my natural blackness is changed
into the beauty of the heavenly King.

O the burning of the fire!
Infinitely burning above all other fires!
How infinitely you burn me,
and the more you burn me the sweeter you are to me.
'O delicious wound',
more delicious to me than all the delights of the world.
'O tender hand',
infinitely more tender than all tenderness,
and the greater the pressure the more tender to me.
'O gentle touch',
the gentleness of which surpasses all the gentleness
and loveliness of created things,
sweeter and more delicious than honey and the honeycomb,
savouring of everlasting life;
and the more profoundly you touch me
the more I taste it.
You are infinitely more precious to me
than gold and precious stones,
for you pay debts which nothing else can pay
because you change death into life.

In this perfect state of life
the soul is, as it were, keeping a perpetual feast
with the praises of God in its mouth,
with a new song of joy and love,
for it knows its high dignity.
Sometimes it glories in repeating the words of Job,
'My glory will be renewed', and
'as a palm tree' I 'shall multiply my days'. (Job 29:18, 20)
That is, God will not permit my glory to diminish as before,
and he will multiply my merits

30

as a palm tree multiplies its branches.
This state is inaccessible to pain, so the soul sings with David,
'You have turned my mourning into dancing,
you have stripped off my sackcloth and wrapped me in gladness;
and now my heart, silent no longer, will play you music;
Yahweh my God, I will praise you forever'. (Ps. 30:10-12)

Here the soul is conscious of God's solicitude to comfort it,
feeling that he himself is encouraging it with tender words;
that he is conferring innumerable graces upon it.
Indeed it seems that there were no other soul in the world
for God to comfort,
no other object of his care,
but that everything was done for this soul alone.

This truly is admitted by the bride in the Canticle
where she says, 'My Beloved is mine and I am his'. (Sg. 2:16)

III

O lamps of fire
In whose splendours
The deep caverns of sense,
Usually dim and dark,
Now with unwonted brightness
Give light and heat together to the Beloved.

I stand in need of God's great help
to enter into the deep meaning of this stanza.
The reader too will need to pay real attention,
for if he or she has not experienced what I speak about
it will seem full of obscurity.
If, on the other hand, one has experienced it,
it will be clear and full of joy.

The bride-soul thanks the Bridegroom from her inmost heart
for all she has received in the state of union.
All the powers of her soul are illumined by the fires of love,
and in response offer that very light and love
to him who has kindled and inspired them.
For one who truly loves is only satisfied
when his whole self, all he is and can be,
are spent in the service of the one he loves.
The greater the service he can render,
the greater his pleasure in giving it.
Such is the joy of the soul now
because it can shine in the presence of the Beloved
with the splendours with which he has surrounded it,
and can love him with the love communicated to it.

O lamps of fire.

Lamps have two properties: they burn and give light.

32

In understanding this stanza we must remember
that God in his one essence contains many attributes,
some known to us, others unknown.
He is omnipotent, wise, good, merciful, just, strong and loving.
And as he reveals himself to the soul
the soul beholds all, by faith, in one simple Essence.
And as each attribute contains the very essence of God,
who is Trinity in Unity,
and as God is infinite light and infinite divine Fire,
it follows that he gives light and burns as true God
in each one of his attributes.
Therefore the knowledge of him to the soul in union
is like that of many lamps,
each lamp, in its own way, radiating love,
and yet all are one substance, all one lamp.
This lamp is all lamps because it gives light
and burns in all ways.

These lamps were seen by Moses on Mount Sinai
where God passed before him
and Moses threw himself on the earth in all haste.
He mentions some of the grandeurs of God which he beheld
and, loving him in them, speaks of them separately in these words:
'Yahweh, Yahweh, a God of tenderness and compassion,
slow to anger, rich in kindness and faithfulness;
for thousands he maintains his kindness,
forgives faults, transgressions, sins;
yet he lets nothing go unchecked'. (Ex. 34:6)
It appears that the principle attributes of God
which Moses then recognised and loved
were those of dominion, onmipotence, mercy, justice and truth.
This is a most profound knowledge
and the deepest delight of love.

It follows that the joy and rapture of love
communicated to the soul in the fire and light of these lamps
is admirable and immeasureable.
It is as if each and all burn with light and fire,

34

making but one light and one fire.

Thus the Spouse who abides in you,
being omnipotent gives himself to you
and loves you omnipotently;
being wise he loves you with wisdom;
being holy he loves you with holiness.
And as he is liberal
you will also feel that he loves you with liberality,
without self-interest, only wanting to do good to you;
showing his countenance joyfully and graciously, saying,
'I am yours and all for you.
It is my pleasure to be what I am
to give myself to you and to be all yours'.

How then can I describe your feelings, O blessed soul,
when you see yourself thus loved and so highly honoured?
You are tasting the bread of life
and are girded about with virtues.
You are delighted with the fragrance of the knowledge of God
which he himself gives you.
This knowledge is infused into you so that you become
'a well of living water,
streams flowing down from Lebanon' (Sg. 4:15)
(Here Lebanon stands for God).
Your joy will be marvellously complete
because in you are accomplished the words of the psalmist:
'There is a river whose streams refresh the city of God'. (Ps. 46:4)

O wonder!
The soul is now overflowing with the divine waters
which run from it as from an abundant fountain
'welling up to eternal life'. (Jn. 4:14)
It is true that this communication is in the light and fire
of the lamps of God;
yet the fire is here so sweet that, though infinite,
it is as the waters of life which satisfy the soul,
quenching its thirst with the vehemence the spirit longs for.

35

Thus, though they are lamps of fire,
they are also the living waters of the Spirit.

The Spirit of God, while hidden in the veins of the soul,
is sweet water quenching its spiritual thirst;
but when the soul offers the sacrifice of love
the Spirit is then living lamps of fire.
These are the lamps of the acts of love spoken of by the bride
when she said, 'The lamps thereof are fire and flames' (Sg. 8:6)
The soul speaks thus because it has fruition,
not only as of the waters of wisdom
but also as of the fire of love in an act of love,
saying, 'O lamps of fire'.
All language is ineffectual to express the matter.
If we consider that the soul is now transformed in God
we shall understand in some measure how it is true
that it is also a fountain of living water
boiling and bubbling upwards in the fire of love which is God.

In whose splendours.

The splendours are the communications of the divine lamps
in which the soul shines forth, with all its faculties
enlightened and united in this loving knowledge.
But unlike ordinary lamps which communicate heat from without,
here it is communicated from within.
For the soul is now within the flames of the lamps
and itself transformed in flame.
Flame is nothing else but air inflamed,
for the fire causes the air within it to burn.
Thus the soul and the Holy Spirit together move the soul as fire moves
the air that is burning.

These movements of two in one are, as it were, acts of God
by which he makes the soul glorious.
The motions and vibrations of fire and flame
admit the soul to a foretaste of heavenly glory
which in the life to come will be perfect, unchanging, continuous.

36

There too the soul will see clearly
how God, though appearing to move within it as the flame
yet in himself is motionless,
just as a fire moves not in its centre.

The 'splendours' are the great graces and favours
which God gives to the soul.
They are also called 'overshadowings'.
In my opinion these are the greatest and highest graces
which can be bestowed in this life in the way of transformation.

Overshadowing is the throwing of a shadow,
and to throw one's shadow over another signifies protection and
favour.
Thus it was said to the Virgin,
'The power of the Most High will cover you with its shadow',
for the Holy Spirit was to approach her so closely
as to 'come upon' her.
The shadow of every object partakes of its likeness,
for if the object be dense
the shadow too will be dense and dark;
if the object be light, its shadow will be light and clear.
We see this in the shadows of wood and crystal
the former throws a dense shadow, the latter a light one.
In spiritual things too, death is the privation of all things.
Thus the psalmist speaks of 'sitting in the shadow of death'
(Ps. 107:10)
whether it be spiritual or bodily darkness.

But the shadow of life is light:
and if divine, a divine light.
Thus the shadow of beauty will be another beauty
according to the nature and quality of the beauty it is shadow of.
The shadow of strength will be in measure and proportion
to the strength it is shadow of.
The same can be said of the shadow of wisdom.

What then must be the shadow of the Holy Spirit,
the shadow of all his power, might and other attributes,

when he is so near the soul?
He touches the soul, not with his shadow only,
but actually uniting himself to it,
so that the soul can taste the very power, wisdom and glory of God.
All this takes place in clear and lumimous shadows
because the attributes and powers of God are lamps
resplendent and luminous in their own right,
which throw forth shadows resplendent and lumimous,
as many and as one.

The soul beholds the Lord as did the prophet Ezechiel. (cf. Ez. 1:5f)
It rejoices in the glory of God
under the protection of his shadow, for the prophet adds,
'It was something that looked like the glory of Yahweh'. (Ez. 1:28)
O how high is the condition of this happy soul! How exalted!
How it marvels at the visions it has within the limits of faith!
How it is profoundly immersed in these waters of the divine
splendours
where the everlasting Father sends forth irrigating streams
which penetrate both soul and body.

O wonder! the lamps of the divine attributes,
though one in substance, yet burn each distinctly.
O abyss of delights! where riches are gathered in simplicity and unity!
O Divine Wisdom! in you we know many things in one,
for you are the treasury of the Father,
'a reflection of the eternal light,
untarnished mirror or God's active power,
image of his goodness'. (Wis. 7:26)

The deep caverns of sense

The caverns are the powers of the soul: memory, intellect, will,
and their depth is commensurate with their capacity for good,
for nothing less than the infinite can fill them.
What they suffer when they are empty
shows in some measure the greatness of their delight
when they are full of God,

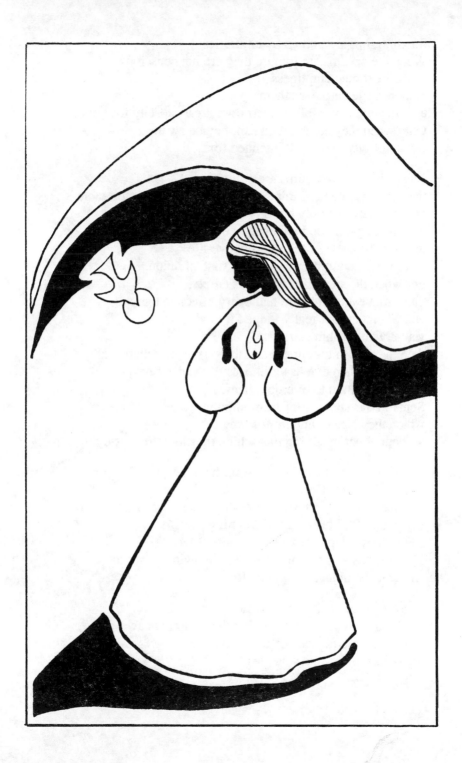

for contraries are known by contraries.
When the caverns are impure they are not conscious
of their extreme emptiness.
A mere trifle perplexes them
and they are insensible to their own great capacity for good.
Only when they are emptied can they be aware
of the infinity they were intended for.

Thus when these caverns are empty
their spiritual hunger, thirst and anxiety become intolerable
because they can only be fully satisfied with God.
This feeling of deep pain usually occurs
towards the close of the illuminative life
and the purgation previous to the state of union.
For when the spiritual appetite is empty,
pure from every creature and every affection thereto;
and when the soul really longs for God
yet he witholds himself,
then the pain of emptiness and thirst is greater than death,
especially when one has glimpses of the divine rays
but cannot attain to or enjoy them.
Souls in this state suffer from impatient love,
which they cannot endure for long
without either receiving that which they long for - or dying.

The emptiness of the first cavern, the intellect,
is the thirst after God.
So great is this thirst that the psalmist compares it to a hart
saying; 'as the hart longs for running streams
so my heart longs for you my God'. (Ps. 42:1)
This thirst is a thirst for the waters of divine Wisdom,
which is the object of the intellect.

The emptiness of the second cavern, the will,
is a hunger for God so great that the soul faints away.
This hunger is for the perfection of love,
the object of the soul's desires.

The emptiness of the third cavern, the memory,
is the soul's languishing for the enjoyment of God;
'My spirit ponders continually and languishes within me.
This is what I shall tell my heart and so recover hope'. (Lam. 3:20,21)

Great then is the capacity of these caverns
because they are capable of containing the infinite God.
Their capacity, and therefore their hunger and thirst,
are in a sense infinite,
their languishing and pain likewise infinite.
In pain the soul is prepared to receive the fulness of God;
but in this life, love does not alleviate the pain,
because the soul is impatient for the full fruition of God,
for which it hopes with intense desire.

But if the one who truly longs for God
is in some sense already in possession of him
why is there pain?
Because there is a great difference between
the fruition of God by grace alone
and the fruition of him in union.
The difference resembles that between espousals and marriage.
The former implies only agreement and mutual good will,
contracted with bridal presents, visits,
and the ornaments graciously given by the bridegroom.
But there is still no personal union
although the espousals are for this end.
When the soul has been completely purified
it is one with the will of God;
it has attained to the state of betrothal
and has the fruition of God by grace.
The Word, the Bridegroom, visits the soul often,
with loving comfort and delight.
But all this admits of no comparison
with that which belongs to the state of spiritual marriage.

Now though it is true this takes place in the soul
when it is perfectly purged of all created affection

41

(and this must take place before the spiritual espousals)
time is still needed for the consummation of the spiritual marriage.
We have a type of this in the book of Esther
where the virgins to be presented to the king
were kept in the palace for a whole year:
'This preparatory period was occupied as follows:
six months with oil of myrrh
six months with spices and lotions' (Est. 2:12)
after which they could appear in the king's presence.

During the time of espousals, and in expectation of the spiritual marriage,
the unction of the Spirit disposing the soul for union is most penetrating,
and the longing of the caverns for fulfilment
becomes more pressing and keen,
firing the soul with yearnings both deep and delicious.

This would be a good opportunity to warn souls
about those to whom they commit themselves for guidance
on the path to union.
I feel great pain and grief of heart
at the sight of some souls who go backwards;
not only by withdrawing from further anointings of the Spirit
but even losing the effects of what they have already received.

In the first place, if a soul is seeking after God
the Beloved is seeking it much more.
If it sends after him its loving desires which are
'Like a column of smoke, breathing of myrrh and frankincense'
(Sg. 3:6)
he on his part sends forth the odour of his ointments
which draw the soul to run after him.
These ointments are his divine inspirations and touches
which, proceeding from him, are always directed and ordered
by the perfection of the law of God and of the Faith,
in which perfection the soul must be always drawing nearer to God.
The soul must therefore recognise

42

that all it is given in the unctions and odours of God
are to dispose it for another and higher unction,
until it is able to be transformed in the divine union.

Since God is the chief agent in this work,
since he is the One who guides and leads the soul,
the soul must take care not to put obstacles in the way,
so that the Holy Spirit may lead it unimpeded along the road
which is the law of God and the Faith.
Difficulties will ensue if the soul entrusts itself to blind guides
three of which can easily lead it astray:
the spiritual director, the devil and the self.

As to the first, it is of the greatest importance
that the soul who wishes to advance in perfection
consider carefully to whom it entrusts itself.
For as the master so is the disciple, as the father so is the child.
Learned directors are few, and they need prudence and experience.
Though the foundations of good directors are learning and discretion,
yet if they are themselves inexperienced in the higher ways
they do not know how to guide others along them,
and can therefore inflict great harm on their penitents.
They do this by guiding souls along paths they have only read about
and which are adapted only for beginners.

The state of beginners is one of meditation and reflection,
accustoming the senses and desires to good things,
so that souls may be detached from the things of this world
through the sweetness they discover in heavenly things.
When this has been done
God begins to introduce the soul into the state of contemplation.
This happens quite quickly when people have entered religious life.
They have therefore to pass on from meditation to contemplation.
This begins when discursive meditation fails,
when sensible sweetness and first fervour ceases,
and the soul falls into aridity.
God is now working in a special manner not discernible to the senses,
infusing knowledge and teaching the soul in his own way.

At this time then, the direction of the soul
must be wholly different from what it was at first.
Formerly it could meditate; now it cannot do so.
However hard it tries, only distractions result.
The soul has to renounce all desire for sweetness and fervour
which it cannot recover by its own efforts.
It must allow God to guide it in secret
without falling back on the operations of sense.
This is because the senses have ceased to be the channels
of spiritual good.
Souls in this state should not be forced to meditate,
nor to apply themselves to discursive reflections,
nor to strive after feelings of sweetness and fervour.
To do this is to place obstacles in the way of the Holy Spirit.
For it is now God himself
who is quietly infusing wisdom and knowledge into the soul,
independently of a multiplicity of acts.
The soul must be as it were passive, making no efforts of its own but
be purely, simply and lovingly intent upon God.
God is simply giving - the soul must simply receive.
The receiver therefore must adapt himself to the gift
that the gift may be accepted and preserved as it is given.

At this point the soul must abstain from its former meditations
and encourage a disposition of passive, loving attention,
submissive and calm.
Otherwise it will place a barrier against the graces
which God wishes to give in the way of loving knowledge.
To be the recipient of God's graces as he wishes to give them
the soul must be perfectly detached, calm, peaceful and serene.
It must be like the atmosphere
which the sun warms and illumines in proportion to its calmness and
purity.

Thus the soul must be attached to nothing,
 not even to the subject of its meditation, nor to spiritual sweetness.
God requires that the spirit be free,
profoundly silent,

44

so as to be attuned to the deep and delicate voice of God.
He speaks to the heart in solitude,
and the soul must listen to him in profound peace and tranquillity.
It must be completely self-forgetful,
wholly intent upon hearing,
free and ready to act on whatever the Lord requires from it.

To contemplate is to receive,
and it is impossible to receive the highest wisdom
unless one is silent and detached
from all sweetness, particular knowledge and personal liking.
Take the mote and film from your eye and make it clean,
then the sun will shine for you
and enable you to see clearly.
Establish your soul in freedom and peace,
withdraw from the yoke and slavery of your own efforts
and move towards the promised land flowing with milk and honey.
In the wilderness, God will supply manna
'containing every delight, satisfying every taste' (Wis. 16:20)
as long as you encourage no other desire save for this food.

Strive therefore to root out of the soul
all desire for sweetness, all efforts after meditation;
establish yourself in estrangement from all around you
and remain in solitude.
The soul in this state feels a certain alienation,
it inclines to solitude
and a sense of weariness in the things of the world;
for when we taste of the spirit the flesh becomes insipid.
Meanwhile the unction of the Holy Spirit
is secretly poured upon the soul
and it is secretly filled with gifts and graces.
God, who accomplishes this, works as God and in a way only he can.

This subtle work of God, imperceptible to both soul and director,
is hindered by any application of sense and desire.
The evil goes unperceived and its cause is miniscule,
yet it inflicts a great stain on one striving for pureness,

and harms it more than it would one who has not attained
such a high degree of perfection.
It is as if a beautiful painting were roughly handled
and smeared with coarse and vile colours.
The injury done is greater, more observable and deplorable
than it would be if a multitude of common paintings were so treated.

An inexperienced spiritual director works like a rough blacksmith
on souls called to greater contemplation. He says:
'Come, get rid of this waste of time, this idleness,
arise and meditate; make interior acts;
it is necessary to make diligent efforts of your own,
everything else is but delusion and foolishness'.
Such a director does not understand
that the soul has passed beyond that state
and is under the direct influence of God.
Let directors remember that the Holy Spirit is the principal agent
and the real guide of souls.
He never ceases to take care of them
and draw them closer to God by the quickest route.
Therefore spiritual directors should remember
that they are only instruments
and must guide those entrusted to them
according to the spirit which God gives to each.
They are not to dragoon people along a path of their own choosing
but to ascertain how the Lord himself is guiding their penitents.
If they are unable to discern this
let them leave souls alone and not disquiet them.
Let them adapt their instructions to the directions of God
and try to lead their penitents into greater solitude, liberty and
tranquillity,
so that their spirit may not be tied down to any particular course,
for God himself is leading them on.
If the soul remains empty and pure,
then, as the rising sun shines into your house
if you but open the windows,
so God, the 'unsleeping keeper of Israel',
will shine upon the emptied soul and fill it with good things

Directors must help lay the foundations of Gospel perfection,
but let them not proceed to the actual building
for 'If Yahweh does not build the house
in vain the masons toil'. (Ps. 127:1)
As he is the supernatural builder
he will build every soul according to his own good pleasure.
As a person advances, so the more does he walk by faith.
He believes without seeing;
he draws nearer to God by not understanding than by understanding.
In fact, to advance *is* to walk more and more by faith.

In contemplation both knowledge and love
are indistinct and general,
sometimes one then the other predominating.
God infuses love into the soul, kindling it with his fire.
The soul therefore must be completely detached
not seeking any kind of consolation without,
even though it feels none in God within either.
The precept of love is to love God above all things,
and if love is to be perfect
we must live in perfect detachment and emptiness.
As regards the imagination - it is of no use here either
for God is far beyond and above anything we can imagine.
So it is a mistake for directors
to instruct their penitents to meditate imaginatively;
this will only result in dryness and repugnance,
for the time for meditation is passed.
To try to return to it destroys all peace of soul,
for God is feeding the spirit, not the senses.

How precious in God's sight is this sleep of the senses
as the Canticle says:
'I charge you, daughters of Jerusalem,
by the gazelles, by the hinds of the field,
not to stir my love, nor rouse it,
until it please to awake'. (Sg. 3:5)
Therefore directors should not stir souls to labour
but allow God to do his own work;

48

otherwise the vineyard is harrassed
and the little foxes that destroy the vines are not driven away.

Incompetent directors, who have little knowledge,
ought to be humble
and direct advanced souls to those who understand them
and can give proper advice.
The carving, finishing and painting of an image
takes a variety of skills,
not every workman can perform them all perfectly,
for delicate work requires a delicate touch.
Therefore a director must be ready to pass his penitents on to others
who have deeper knowledge.
He must not try to hold on to them for his own advantage
as if he were a jealous husband.
Souls must be left sovereignly free to follow the Lord
as he guides them.
To directors who do not attend to this truth God says:
'Trouble to the shepherds of Israel . . .
you have fed on milk, you have dressed yourselves in wool . . .
but failed to feed the flock . . .
so I am going to call the shepherds to account'. (Ez. 34:2, 10)
Penitents must always be allowed to seek other advice
and not feel their directors are displeased if they do.

Another factor which directors use to their advantage
and which is worse than the plague
is to deter penitents from entering the religious life,
by counselling delay and suggesting difficulties.
They thus take good thoughts away from the hearts of those who
consult them.
These directors have not passed through the 'strait gate'
nor will they allow others to do so.
These are they whom our Lord threatens in the gospel saying:
'Woe to you lawyers who have taken away the key of knowledge!
You have not gone in yourselves
and have prevented others from going in who wanted to'. (Lk. 11:52)
Such directors advise contrary to the gospel

and are blind guides, leading souls away from the Holy Spirit.

The other blind guide to the soul at this stage is Satan.
He hates and envies the soul anointed by the Holy Spirit
and tries to entice it back to the ways of sweetness,
withdrawing it from solitude and deep recollection.
The soul then feels that the way of sweetness is preferable
and, for a mouthful of this food,
disqualifies itself from feeding upon God;
for God was offering himself as its nourishment.

The evil spirit thus inflicts great evils upon souls;
with a trifling bait dragging them forth like fish
from the depths of the pure waters of the Spirit
where they were engulfed and drowned in God,
relying upon no created support.
The soul, thinking this is God's visitation
and therefore a great gain,
omits to enter the inner chamber of the Bridegroom
and stands at the door
to see what is passing in the exterior part of itself.
Satan too sometimes tries to draw the soul from recollection
by tumults and fears of one kind or another,
endeavouring to make it fix its attention upon self
and thus lose its precious graces.
But if Satan fails in these efforts
he departs and leaves the soul alone.

O souls, now that God shows you mercies so great,
leading you into solitude and recollection
and withdrawing you from the labours of sense,
do not try to return to them.
The senses were indeed profitable at the beginning
and enabled you to deny yourself in many things.
But at this stage God himself has begun to work in you.
If therefore you are careful to lay no stress on your own senses,
withdrawing them from all things,
involving them with nothing,

waiting lovingly and sincerely on God,
doing no violence to yourself
apart from detaching yourself wholly from all things
so as not to disturb your inner peace and tranquillity,
God himself will feed you with heavenly food
since you have ceased to hinder him.

The third blind guide of the soul is the soul itself
who, not understanding its state, disturbs and injures itself
by striving to elicit acts as previously.
The consequence of this is distraction, aridity and disgust,
where before the soul delighted in the calm peace and silence
wherein God himself was secretly infusing his sweetness.
It sometimes happens that God persists
in keeping the soul in this quiet calm
and yet the soul persists in crying out with the imagination
and in walking with the intellect.
Such souls are like children in their mother's arms
who, unable to walk, cry and struggle with their feet,
demanding to be allowed to walk unaided;
yet who cannot walk by themselves
and suffer not their mothers to do so either.
These souls make God resemble a painter whose work is hindered
because the subject he is portraying
refuses to remain stationary.

The soul should here keep in mind
that it is now making greater progress
than it could do by any efforts of its own,
even though it be wholly unconscious of that progress.
God himself is carrying it in his arms
and thus it is not aware of advancing.
Though it thinks it is doing nothing, yet in truth more is done
than if the soul itself were the agent,
for it is God who is at work.
If this work is invisible that is nothing remarkable,
for the work of God in the soul
is wrought silently and unknown to the senses.

Let the soul then abandon itself to the hands of God
and trust in him.
Whoever does that advances securely
for there is only danger when we try to act on our own strength.

Let us now return to the deep caverns of the faculties
in which, as I said, the sufferings of the soul are usually great
when God is anointing it and preparing it for union with himself
by subtle and delicate unctions.
These penetrate into the immense void of its caverns
filling the depths of the soul with sweetness
and disposing it for the divine union.

Now if the unction which prepares the soul is so wonderful,
what will the spiritual marriage be like?
It is surely certain that then the hunger and thirst of the caverns
will be satisfied with fulness and delight.

Dim and dark.

The eye is unable to see for either of two reasons:
it is in darkness or it is blind.
God is the light and the true object of the soul;
when he does not shine upon it it is in darkness
even though its vision may be faultless.
When the soul is in sin,
or when it occupies the desires with things other than God,
it is then blind.
Though the light of God be not wanting to it
yet, being blind, it cannot see the light;
and its blindness is the practical ignorance in which it lives.
Before God enlightened the soul in its transformation
it was in darkness and ignorance of his great goodness,
as was the Wise Man before he was enlightened,
for he says, 'He enlightened my ignorance'.

Spiritually speaking, it is one thing to be blind,
another to be in darkness.

52

Blindness proceeds from sin, darkness not necessarily so.
There is natural darkness where light does not shine
and there is supernatural darkness
where there is no knowledge of many supernatural things.
Without God the intellect abides in darkness
for until God said 'let there be light',
darkness was upon the face of the deep of the caverns of the souls's senses.
The deeper the cavern where God does not shine
the deeper is the darkness.
Thus it is impossible to lift the eyes to the divine light
for it is not even thought of.
It is not known to exist and therefore is not desired.
In this case the soul desires darkness rather than light
and so goes from darkness to darkness,
for darkness only guides the soul to greater darkness,
as like calls forth like.
Likewise the light of grace given to the soul
which opens it to the divine light
and makes it pleasing to God
calls to another deep of grace - the divine transformation
wherein the eye of sense is enlightened and made acceptable.

The mind was also blind when it took pleasure in other than God.
Desires cloud the eye of reason
and prevent it from seeing what is before it.
Thus the grandeur and magnificence of the divine beauty
are rendered invisible when the sense pleasures are followed.
For if the eye is covered, even with a tiny object,
that is enough to obstruct its vision
even if what is before it is enormous.
Thus a single desire fostered by the soul
is sufficient to impede the sight of all the divine grandeurs
which are beyond its desires and longings.
O how impossible it is for a soul subject to desires
to judge rightly of the things of God!
One cannot judge desires aright when under their influence.
Instead one comes to consider the things of God not to be God's,

and the things which are not God's to be his.

While this cloud and cataract cover the eye of judgement
nothing is visible apart from the cloud,
which is sometimes one colour, sometimes another, according to
circumstances.
And people take the cloud to be God
because that is all they can see, for it overshadows the senses
and God is not comprehended by sense.
Thus desire and sensual satisfaction hinder the knowledge of high
things,
for 'the fascination of evil throws good things into shade
and the whirlwind of desire corrupts a simple heart'. (Wis. 4:12)
Those persons who are not so spiritually advanced
as to be purified from all their desires and inclinations
often believe things to be important
which are of no account in spirituality,
and are in fact closely tied to the things of sense;
as it is written, 'An unspiritual person
is one who does not accept anything of the Spirit of God:
he sees it all as nonsense; it is beyond his understanding
because it can only be understood by means of the Spirit'. (1 Cor. 2:14)

The 'sensual' person
is one who lives according to natural desires.
Even though these natural desires sometimes come into contact
with things of the spirit, yet if one cleaves to spiritual things
with natural desires they are still only natural.
The spirituality of the object counts for little
if the desire for it proceeds from and is rooted in nature.
What! you will exclaim, is it not supernatural desire to desire God?
No, not always.
It is so only when the motive is supernatural
and the strength of the desire proceeds from God.
When the desire comes from yourself it is merely natural.
Therefore your perception and judgement are faulty,
for what is spiritual transcends all natural sense and desire.

If you still doubt the truth of what I say
read over again what I have written and perhaps your doubts will
vanish.
Before this, the sense of the soul, obscure without the divine light,
and blinded by its desires,
is now such that because of the divine union
its deep caverns 'give light and heat together to the Beloved'.

With unwonted brightness give light and heat together to the Beloved

These caverns of the soul's faculties
being now among the marvellous splendours
of the lamps which burn within them,
being lighted and burning in God,
remit back to God in God, in addition to their self-surrender,
those very splendours which they receive from him in living glory.
They also, turning to God in God,
being themselves lamps burning in the brightness of the divine lamps
return to the Beloved that very light and warmth of love
which they received from him.
Now indeed they give back to him, in the way they received them,
those very splendours which he communicated,
as a crystal reflects the rays of the sun when shone upon.

'With unwonted brightness'
that is, strange and surpassing all imagination and description.
For the perfection of beauty in the soul
restores to God what it has received from him.
The intellect, made one with God, receives the divine wisdom,
the will, in complete conformity with God's will,
is as one with him.
In the same way, in proportion as it knows God's greatness
and is united with it,
the soul shines and radiates the warmth of love.
And according to the other divine attributes communicated to it
the soul gives back such things as strength, beauty, justice,
giving them to the Beloved in the very light and heat
they receive from him.

56

The soul, now being one with God,
is itself God by participation.
Though it is not as perfect as it will be in the world to come
it is still God in a shadow.
Thus, by reason of its transformation,
and being a shadow of God,
it gives and reflects God back to himself.
Being united to him in will, the soul seems in truth to possess God.
It possesses him as his adopted child, by right of ownership,
by the free gift he has made of himself to it.
Here every debt is paid,
for the soul gives freely, with inestimable joy and delight,
giving the Holy Spirit as its own, of its own free will,
so that God may be loved as he deserves to be.

Herein consists the inestimable joy of the soul,
for it sees that it offers God what is worthy of him - his own being.
Though it is true that God cannot be given anything new,
God is indeed repaid by this gift of the soul.
He receives the gift of the soul as if it were its own,
and in the giving he loves it anew, gives himself to it anew,
and the soul reciprocates the love anew.
Thus there is a mutual interchange of love between the soul and God
in the conformity of their union and in matrimonial surrender.
Each give themselves up to the other
and can say to each other what the Son said to the Father,
'All I have is yours and all you have is mine
and in them I am glorified'. (Jn. 17:10)
This will be verified in fruition in the next life,
and is verified too in the state of union
which God energises in an act of love.

The soul can offer such gifts which are far greater than itself,
just as a ruler can offer kingdoms and nations
to whomever he will.
This is the cause of the soul's happiness;
that it can give God far more than it is worth in itself,
in fact it can give God the warmth and light of his own love,

with the liberality which God himself has given. .
This is effected in the life to come
through the light of glory and of love;
it is effected in this present life by enlightened faith and enkindled
love.
Thus the deep caverns of sense
with unwonted brightness give light and heat together to the Beloved.
Together - because the communication
of the Father, the Son and the Holy Spirit in the soul are one;
and they are the light and fire of the love within it.

With respect to love, the soul stands before God in strange beauty.
It loves God by means of God,
because the Holy Spirit within it, who inflames the soul,
loves as the Father loves the Son, as it is written,
'so that the love with which you loved me may be in them,
and so that I may be in them'. (Jn. 17:26)

The second perfection is to love God in God,
for in this union the soul is vehemently absorbed in the love of God
and God communicates himself with great vehemence to the soul.

The third perfection of beauty is that the soul now loves God
for what he is, not merely because he is bountiful, good or generous
to the receiver, but rather because
he is all this essentially in himself.

There are also three perfections of beauty
with respect to that shadow of fruition
which is caused by the union of the intellect and affections in God.
First, the soul enjoys God here, united with God himself,
for, as the soul unites its intellect with wisdom and goodness
and perceives clearly - though not so clearly as in the life to come -
it delights greatly in all these things clearly understood.
The second principal perfection of beauty
is that the soul delights itself in God alone
without the admixture of any created thing.
The third is that it enjoys him alone for what he is
without the admixture of any selfish feeling or created object.

58

IV

How gently and how lovingly
You lie awake in my heart
Where you dwell secretly and alone;
And in your sweet breathing
Full of grace and glory
How tenderly you fill me with love.

Here the soul turns towards the Bridegroom with great love
praising and thanking him for two marvellous acts
which he sometimes effects in the soul through its union with himself.
The soul too observes the way he produces them
and their effects upon itself.

The first effect is the awakening of God in the soul,
and the way of that is gentleness and love.
The second is the breathing of God in the soul
and the way of that is grace and glory given in breathing.
The effect of this is to make the soul
love God sweetly and tenderly.
The stanza may therefore be paraphrased as follows:
O how gently and lovingly you lie awake in the centre of my soul
where you dwell secretly and alone in silence.
You abide in me as my sole Lord
not only as if in your own house and your own room
but also within my heart in close and intimate union.
O how gently and how lovingly!
Sweet to me is your breathing in that awakening
for it is full of grace and glory.
O with what tenderness you inspire me to love you!
The metaphor is borrowed from one awaking from sleep
and drawing his breath
for the soul in this state feels it to be so.

The awakenings of God in the soul are so many
that were I to describe them I would never end.
The awakening the soul refers to here, the work of the Son of God,
is, in my opinion, of the highest kind
and the source of the greatest good in the soul.
This awakening is a movement of the Word
in the depths of the soul;
an awakening of such grandeur, authority and glory,
and of such profound sweetness
that all the balsams, aromatic herbs and flowers of the world
seem to be mingled and shaken together
for the production of sweetness,
and all the kingdoms and dominions of the world,
all the powers and virtues of heaven, seem to be moved.
This is not all, for all the virtues, substance, perfections and graces
of all created things shine forth
and make the same movement together.
For as St John says, 'all that came to be had life in him' (Jn. 1:3)
and in him moves and lives; as the apostle says,
'In him we live and move and exist'. (Acts 17:28)

The reason is this:
when the grand Emperor wills to reveal himself to the soul,
because he bears all creation within him
it moves when he does.
For when he comes, moving yet unmoving,
he bears his whole court as does a prince.
This however is a very imperfect illustration;
for here things not only seem to move
but also reveal the beauty, power, loveliness of their being,
rooted in him from whom they draw life.
Here indeed the soul understands
how all creatures live, continue and draw life from him,
and so it understands the meaning of these words,
'By me monarchs rule and princes issue just laws,
by me rulers govern, and the great impose justice on the world'.

(Prov. 8:15, 16)

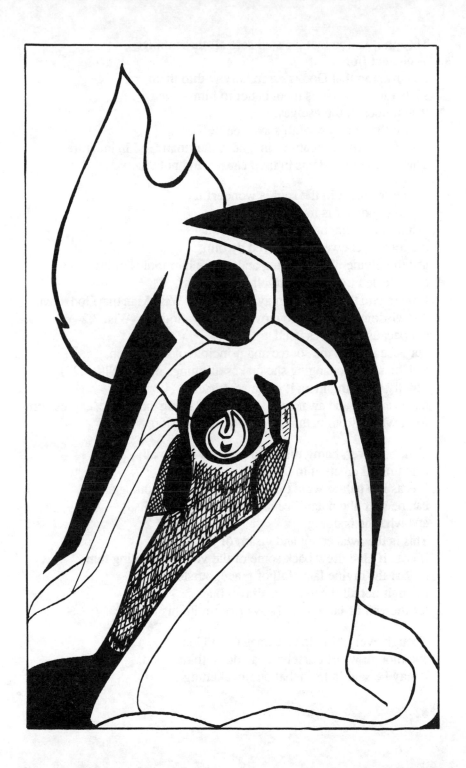

Though it is true that the soul sees all these things
as distinct from God
it knows too that God is essentially within them,
so that it understands them better in him
than it does in themselves.
Hence the great joy of this awakening -
namely, to know creatures in God rather than God in creatures.
This is to know effects in their causes and not vice versa.

This movement in the soul is wonderful
for God himself is immovable.
Without movement on the part of God
the soul is renewed and moved by him;
and the divine life and being and all the harmonies of creation
are revealed to it with marvellous newness.
If we regard the effect we may say with the Wise Man that God moves
'for wisdom is quicker to move than any motion', (Wis. 7:24)
not because it moves itself
but because it is the source and principle of all motion,
and 'herself unchanging she makes all things new'. (Wis. 7:27)
Strictly speaking then, it is the soul itself
that is moved and awakened, 'awakened' being the correct expression
for it wakes from natural to supernatural vision.

God, however, being ruler and giver of life to all,
contains all creation in himself.
It is as if a palace were thrown open, so that at one glance
can be seen the magnificence of him who inhabits it
and what he is doing.
This is the awakening and vision of the soul.
It is as if God drew back some of the veils concealing him
so that the divine face, full of grace, bursts forth;
(though not all the veils are drawn back
for the veil of faith will always remain in this life.)

Though everything in us comes from God,
and though we of ourselves can do nothing good,
it may be said in truth that our awakening

62

is the very awakening of God, and our rising the rising of God.
'Wake up, Lord! Why do you sleep?' says the psalmist.
In other words: Raise us up and wake us for we have fallen asleep.
Thus, because the soul could never rouse and awaken itself
but must rely on God to do so,
its awakening is most properly referred to God:
'You lie awake in my heart'.

You lie awake in my heart.

Awake and enlighten us, Lord,
that we may know and love the good things you have set before us,
that we may know that you wish to do us good
and remember us always.
It is utterly impossible to describe what the soul in this awakening
knows and feels of the goodness of God
in the inmost depths of its being - its heart.
For deep within the soul resounds an infinite power,
sweet and gracious in the Lord, who holds within himself
all the sweetness and graces of his creation.

But how can the soul bear all this while still in the flesh,
when it has not the strength necessary and seems to be fainting away?
The very sight of Ahasuerus on his throne, in his glittering robe,
was so terrible in the eyes of Esther
that she fainted through fear when she gazed on his face.
'My Lord', she said, 'you looked to me like an angel of God,
and my heart was moved with fear of your majesty'. (Est. 15:10)
Glory oppresses the one who beholds it
if he is not made glorious by it in his turn.
How much more, then, is the soul liable to faint away
when it beholds not just an angel but the Lord of angels,
with his face full of the beauty of all creatures,
terrible in power and glory, and bearing innumerable excellences.
It is to this Job referred when he said,
'a whispered echo is all we hear of him,
but who could comprehend the thunder of his power?' (Job 26:14)

63

The soul, however, does not faint away and tremble at this glorious awakening,
for it is now in the state of perfection
and its lower nature is conformed to the higher part of the spirit.
Also, although God shows his greatness and glory,
he does so gently and lovingly,
comforting, exalting and sustaining the soul.
This is easy enough to him who, with his right hand,
protected Moses so that he might behold his glory (cf. Ex. 33:22)

Thus the soul feels God's love and gentleness
to be one with his power, authority and greatness.
Therefore the soul is strengthened to sustain its deep joy.
Esther indeed fainted away when the king seemed unfavourable towards her,
but the moment he beheld her graciously,
touched her with his sceptre and kissed her,
she recovered herself, for he said then,
'I am your brother, have no fear'.
So it is with the soul in the presence of the King of kings.
The moment he shows himself as Spouse and Brother
all fear vanishes.
Showing the soul his power, love and goodness,
in gentleness rather than in anger,
he communicates to it the love in his own breast,
'leaping from his throne' to caress it as a bridegroom,
touching it with the sceptre of his majesty,
embracing it as a brother.
There the royal robes and the fragrance thereof,
which are the marvellous attributes of God,
there the splendour of gold, which is charity,
and the glittering of the precious stones of supernatural knowledge,
and there the face of the Word full of grace,
strike the queenly soul, so that, transformed in the virtues of the King,
it beholds itself a queen. Thus the psalmist can say in truth:
'On your right stands the queen in gold of Ophir'. (Ps. 45:9)
All this passes in the very depths of the soul;
so it immediately adds, 'Where you dwell secretly and alone'.

Where you dwell secretly and alone

God is said to dwell secretly in the soul's very heart
because this sweet embrace takes place
in the inmost substance and powers of the soul.
We must keep in mind that God dwells in secret and hidden ways
in all souls, in their very substance,
for if he did not they could not exist at all.
This dwelling of God is very different in different souls.
In some he dwells alone, in others not;
in some he dwells contented, in others displeased;
in some as in his own house, ordering and ruling it,
in others as a stranger in a house not his own,
where he is not permitted to command or do anything at all.
Where personal desires and self-will least abound
there he is most alone and contented;
there he dwells as in his own house, ruling and directing it,
and the more secretly he dwells the more he is alone.

So then, in the soul where no desires dwell,
which has cast out all images and forms of created things,
the Beloved himself dwells most secretly;
and the purer the soul, the greater its estrangment from all that is not
God,
the more intimate his converse and the closer his embrace.
Thus he dwells in a secrecy not even Satan can penetrate.
Only the soul is conscious of his presence.

O how blessed is that soul
ever conscious of God resting and reposing within it!
How necessary it is for such a soul
to flee from the matters of this world and live in great tranquillity
so that nothing whatever may disturb the Beloved at his repose.
He is there as it were asleep in the embraces of the soul,
and the soul is, in general, conscious of his presence
and has fruition of him most deeply.
If he were always awake in the soul
the communications of knowledge and love would be unceasing

and that would be the state of glory.
If but *one* awakening can affect the soul so profoundly
what would become of it if God continually awake within it?

In other souls which have not yet attained to this state of union
he also dwells secretly.
Such souls are not generally conscious of his presence
but only so in the time of these sweet awakenings,
which are not the same as those already described,
nor can they be compared to them.
The senses are not wholly ordered, and are therefore excitable,
so the soul by its outward demeanour
indicates its state to the devil.
But in the awakening of the perfect soul by the Bridegroom
all is perfect, because effected by the Bridegroom himself.
In this awakening, as of one aroused from sleep and drawing breath
the soul feels the breathing of God,
there it says, 'in your sweet breathing'.

And in your sweet breathing, full of grace and glory, how tenderly you fill me with love.

I would not speak of this breathing of God,
neither do I wish to do so,
because I am certain that I cannot.
Indeed were I to try it would never approximate the reality.
This aspiration is an act of his in the soul
whereby he breathes into it the Holy Spirit.
This breathing is full of grace and glory
and therefore the Holy Spirit fills the soul with goodness and glory
inspiring it with a love of himself
which transcends all glory and all understanding.
For this reason I must desist from speaking on the subject.